I'm not crazy, I just lost my glasses.

by LONNY SHAVELSON

Introduction by A.D. Coleman
Photography critic and historian
Tisch School of the Arts
New York University

Foreword by Sheldon J. Korchin
Professor and Director
Graduate Program in Clinical Psychology
University of California, Berkeley

I'M NOT CRAZY, I JUST LOST MY GLASSES

This book is available by mail from:

De Novo Press
POB 5106
Berkeley, CA 94705
(415) 849-9382

$12.95 (California residents add sales tax)
$1.00 Shipping

Discounts are available for larger orders and for organizations involved in self-help for those with mental disabilities.

Book design by Lonny Shavelson

Cover design by Lonny Shavelson and Paul Marcus

Printed in the U.S.A. by Phelps/Schaefer Litho-Graphics Co.
Brisbane, California

Typesetting by Generic Typography
Emeryville, California

ISBN #0-912357-01-0

Library of Congress Catalog Card Number: 86-72109

This book is also also available for audiovisual presentation in slide/tape and video format. Contact De Novo Press for details.

Also by Lonny Shavelson
PERSONAL AD PORTRAITS
De Novo Press, 1983

Grateful Acknowledgments: I wish to thank the many photographers and friends who encouraged and tirelessly reviewed this work as it evolved, with special thanks to Chris Johnson and San Francisco Camerawork, Deborah Bickel and Amy Shapiro.

THAT WAY I'LL BE OUT OF THE BLAST ZONE

by A.D. Coleman

I've an old, dear friend who (like his father before him) spent a portion of his life in East Coast mental institutions. Today he and I teach in the same university photography department; his appearance and behavior in no way mark him as different from the rest of us.

That, in fact, was always the problem from my standpoint. The first decade of our friendship was punctuated, arrhythmically, by his disappearance—usually self-imposed—into the mental-health system. Despite my love for him, though he was often only minutes away, I rarely visited him during those internments. The obstacle was this: Except when the healers rendered him inarticulately somnolent with their techniques of chemical stupefaction, he spoke, acted, perceived in the same way whether he was inside or outside.

You see, understanding and empathizing with him in the everyday world was easy. So was doing the same while he was hospitalized—but that raised a series of unnerving questions: What had changed? Why was he in there? And (most terrifyingly) if I could agree with his perceptions, why wasn't I in there with him? The fear evoked by these was enough to overwhelm my affection for and commitment to him; his forgiveness has not erased my memory of that paralysis.

* * * * *

Another friend of mine is fond of asserting that the difference between a psychosis and a culture is merely statistical: "Discover one person in your neighborhood who eats human flesh and you've got a 'certifiable lunatic,'" he says; "find ten thousand like her on a Pacific island and you send in Margaret Mead with a research grant."

Facile as this may sound, it speaks to the central issue of this project of Lonny Shavelson's: We still know little about the condition loosely referred to as insanity—surely not enough to enable us to distinguish readily between the sane and the insane. Nor is this dilemma exclusive to the lay person. As R.D. Laing has written, "There are at present no objective, reliable, quantifiable criteria—behavioural or neurophysiological or biochemical—to appeal to when psychiatrists differ."

After all, a psychiatric diagnosis is at best a hypothesis, a subjective interpretation. When confronted with a human being labelled as somehow psychologically disturbed, the first challenge is overcoming the tendency to make that tentative description into a *thing* which in some way is *in* the person. (This inclination is exacerbated by much psychiatric jargon, such as the description of that abstraction to which the name *neurosis* is attached as "an entity.") Both the lay observer and the psychiatrist must learn to understand behavior as contextually grounded, evolving as a response to the behavior of others. This not only impeaches the isolation-ward approach to psychiatric observation, but proposes as substitutes the metaphors of ecology and general-systems theory.

Understandably, if regrettably, there are pitfalls which snare most of those who deal with madness: acting as if the condition were contagious; conceptualizing it as symptomatic of flaws in the individual rather than dysfunctions in the system(s) of which s/he is part; judging, judging, judging . . .

Yet who—and how—are we to judge the so-called mentally ill? Consider those who choose to stand before us in Shavelson's idiosyncratic cross-section. Some impress me as lucid, cogent, insightful; others—by their ideas, their tones of voice, the expression of their eyes—persuade me that they have stepped out of reach. I suspect that each reader/viewer of this image-text work will have similar reactions—but that the configuration of our responses to any particular individual would be wildly varied.

"I'm not able to put on that social mask that you see, where people look so perfect and whole," one of them confesses, in a self-evaluation whose candor and perceptiveness strike me as signs of rationality. "Barry Manilow was on TV and I was sure he was looking at me. I want more experiences like that," exclaims another; I would consider the search for quality time with Barry Manilow via television a cause hopeless to the point of delusion—yet that singer/songwriter has enough fans with parallel aspirations to constitute the statistical culture of which my sarcastic friend speaks. At what point does a definition of abnormality succumb to the vagaries of mere taste? Obsessive pursuit of an *idee fixe* can get you locked up; it can also get you a Nobel Prize.

In this case, the confusion is compounded by the form itself. Photography, after all, has its limitations. One is that photographs particularize, although we are all too prone to generalize from them. Another is that a photograph describes only the light reflected from the surface of what's before the lens. Nothing more, nothing less.

In a way, then, photography is almost the antithesis of psychiatry; for psychiatry is a discipline which insists that the truths of identity and experience are sub-texts, patterns made accessible by disregarding the seductive veneer of surface. Yet, despite this seeming incompatibility, there is an operative relationship between photography and psychiatry which goes back well over a century, ranging from the attempts by Bertillon and others to create composite typologies and classification systems for criminality and insanity to the increasing use of self-portraiture and family-album imagery in present-day therapeutic practice.

What photography does, it does inimitably. A photograph reveals much about the photographer's response to his/her subject. When the approach is transactional, as it is here—when the subject is aware of photographer and camera, and the relation is consensual—a unique kind of information can be registered on film. In this collaboration (for it is such), if the photographer can avoid intrusive stylistic interjections, the subject has some control over how s/he will appear. If, in combination with the transactional mode, photographer and subject accept an environmental one, setting the subject in a familiar space, it is possible to render a photographic version of what the late sociologist Erving Goffman called "the presentation of self in everyday life."

Shavelson has achieved that here, I think, in a way that is all the more admirable for its self-effacement. Clearly, he has put his collaborators at ease. In part this must be due to his own self-presentation during the photographic sessions, but it may also be attributable to his yielding to his subject's control over many aspects of what we might call the *mise-en-image:* costume, body posture, facial expression, environment. Here there is no covert recording of accidental gestures, no exaggeration of features or setting by shocking proximity or lenticular distortion. These people are given the courtesy of a distance somewhere between the personal and the social, then are granted the right to compose themselves for the camera. The revelations that occur here are, therefore, largely conscious and deliberate—not so much booty looted by the photographer as gifts offered to him and, through him, to us.

There are many ways to photograph, none of them invalid as such. What Shavelson manages here is what the best psychiatrists —and the best friends—seek to do: he looks beyond the labels, the loaded nomenclature of psychiatric evaluation and description, to the lone person in front of his eyes. Individually, the pictures tell us more about his subjects than about the photographer; cumulatively, that says a great deal about Lonny Shavelson.

In an earlier project, *Personal Ad Portraits,* Shavelson explored the ways in which his subjects projected verbal images of themselves (in that case, via "personal" ads in newspapers) in relation to the ways in which they presented themselves to his camera. That same concern is operative in *I'm Not Crazy,*. . . once again. There's much to be extracted from these image-text pairings, which I'm tempted to describe as self-portrayals because Shavelson has become the instrument of his subjects to at least the same degree as they have served his purposes.

I would hope that a book such as this would be of interest to those in all branches of the mental-health profession, for it brings alive and personalizes people who are all too often discussed as diagnoses, symptoms, types, statistics—"patients," "clients," "units." I do see it making a real contribution to the public debate on issues of mental health. In particular, I think it will be of great service to those who—as "significant others," friends, family, lovers of seriously troubled people— need all the help they can get in rehumanizing those whom diagnostic jargon, mixed with societal anxieties, can easily make disappear. I also suspect it will be enormously powerful for those who have ever been (or been diagnosed as) mentally disturbed, for they may find some of their experience mirrored here in ways that will assure them they are not alone.

This book is useful and relevant to such readers because it makes accessible and humanizes the experience of madness and the treatment thereof. That experience is rendered not in the abstract jargon of the would-be healers but in the commonplace language of the wounded, who are brought to us not as statistics or case studies but people with faces and voices of their own, with stories to tell. If it's true, as so many have now argued, that we make our worlds with words, what could be more instructive than attending to the subtle ways in which each of these people, linguistically, shapes a personal universe—unless it is discovering the futility of any attempt to establish some absolute correlation between their appearances, their diagnoses, and their tales? What could be more healing for those who have opened themselves thus to our scrutiny than the knowledge that they are at last being listened to?

Myself, I'd like to have a beer with Darwin Dias, who proclaims that "the whole system is a madness machine." I understand the dilemma of David Corson, the young fellow who speaks of his explosive rage at his father, then segues: "This area is going to be the first place hit in a nuclear war. I'm going to move to a small town, to where my parents live. That way I'll be out of the blast zone."

I want out of the blast zone too. I still don't understand why I wasn't in there with them.

April, 1986
Staten Island, NY

FOREWORD

While visiting an "asylum for the insane," William James is reported to have said, "There but for the grace of God go I." The pioneer and sage of turn-of-the-century American psychology, James was keenly aware of human problems and social inequities. He actively supported Clifford W. Beers, the former mental patient and author of *A Mind That Found Itself* (1908), in his fight for greater understanding and more humane care of the mentally ill. They founded the National Association for Mental Hygiene, which was a vital advocate for those suffering psychological disability.

Over the years, their cause has been taken up by numerous others. There is no question that significant advances have been made in protecting the civil rights of patients, providing more adequate housing, food, and medical care, and limiting physical abuse, exploitation and social degradation, although enormous problems remain in all of these realms.

The mentally ill are still feared and shunned; they are stereotyped and caricatured; they continue to be stigmatized. People may, in principle, support a halfway house or a new community program, but not in their immediate neighborhood and not if it costs too much.

Few are surprised when newspapers report that a "former state hospital patient attacks. . . ." The fact is that the mentally ill are far more often the victims than the perpetrators of crimes. While the public no longer pays an admission fee to see the lunatics at London's Bethlehem Hospital (contracted in British style to Bedlam), the mentally ill remain the butt of jokes and derision. We have become more sensitive to the feelings of other minorities, but no one protested when the President of the United States called the leader of Libya "the madman of the Mediterranean."

Nor are these attitudes limited to the general public, who may have had little contact with (identified) mentally ill people. Relatives and friends of someone suffering a psychotic episode may well turn away from him or her. Too often, unfortunately, some psychiatrists, psychologists, and other professionals charged with helping the mentally ill are less than the caring helpers their patients need. Given the choice, they elect to work with the less seriously disturbed, in office psychotherapy, clinics and similar settings.

In psychiatric hospitals, human contact between patient and staff may be minimal. At the least, it's a dull existence; as Vivian Bard says in this book, "Back to the hospital. Take your medicine and watch T.V." Joyce Kasinsky puts it more strongly: "It's just that hideous fear because you've been there." Patients treated as "cases" or "schizophrenics" lose individuality. Still, many find satisfaction and respect in the clinical relationship, as does Darryl Del Monte, who says, "I'm seeing a psychiatrist now who's tremendous. I feel like I'm speaking to somebody with an intellect who's recognizing that I have the same." It's clear from the comments of the people Shavelson photographed and interviewed that generalizations about "all psychiatrists" are no more true than those about "all patients."

Lightner Witmer, a contemporary of William James who in the 1890s founded the first psychology clinic in an American university, viewed clinical psychology as growing through, *"The study of individuals, one at a time."* Although our concern is to understand principles of human functioning of "people in general," the unique concern of clinical psychology is with "persons in particular." Clinical psychologists, along with other mental health professionals, are dedicated to improving the lot of individuals in psychological distress. To this end, I would argue, we must depend not only on knowledge of human beings in general, nor even on knowledge of social groups, but ultimately on the understanding of how various forces interact in the psychological life of a unique individual.

While psychology may be conceived as either universal or particular, photography—as Coleman also notes—is by its nature particular. The camera portrays an individual in a specific setting in a given moment in time. We can, of course, depart from the concrete reality of the pictured moment to generate abstractions about all or some of humanity, but we leave the visually given at the risk of substituting delusion for reality.

The photographs and accompanying statements in this book are not only artistic creations but also valuable documents for the "study of persons, one at a time." Shavelson pictures his subjects with uncommon perceptiveness, sympathy, and skill. The relation between photographer and subject is clearly collaborative, respectful, and voluntary—as it should also be, but isn't always, in psychological treatment and research.

The people in this book tell their own stories in their own fashion, in words as well as images. They present themselves as they wish to be known; we in turn don't feel as if we are spying on them. In this atmosphere of trust and respect, they talk openly of bizarre behaviors, delusions, and hallucinations, as well as revealing ways they have coped and ways they have been mistreated.

What comes through is how different these people are from one another and how difficult it is to generalize about them. They are all human and suffer problems; some are sicker and some healthier; we can empathize with some more easily and feel their pain or outrage more readily. But I doubt that anyone can read this book and end up doubting the reality and poignancy of mental illness. More likely, as did William James, they will believe that, "There but for the grace of God, go I."

At the University of California in Berkeley, we have shown these pictures and statements to students in our introductory course in clinical and abnormal psychology. It has been a very effective way to show them "cases" as they really are and to make textbook generalizations into living individuals. It was a sobering and much appreciated experience for students, and it inspired thoughtful discussion. I strongly recommend this volume for students of psychology and for workers in all fields concerned with healthy and disturbed human functioning.

I also hope the book finds a wide audience in the general public, especially among the friends and relatives of present or former psychiatric patients. The life of the mentally ill as pictured here is hardly pleasant, but neither is it as grotesque as common beliefs might hold. For those suffering psychological disability the book can also be recommended, if only to remind them that there are sympathetic friends out there working on their behalf.

Sheldon J. Korchin

Professor of Psychology
University of California
Berkeley

September, 1986

"Pa said, 'S'pose he's telling the truth, that fella? The preacher answered, 'he's telling the truth, awright. The truth for him.' "

John Steinbeck
The Grapes of Wrath

"The medicine cut off the voices immediately. I was impressed. But I was still the Messiah."

Brad Lichtenstein, from

I'M NOT CRAZY, I JUST LOST MY GLASSES

Richard Hasher

I would have gotten paranoid schizophrenia even if I hadn't taken LSD. I had a predisposition to it anyway. My fantasies took over my whole life. I looked forward to going to bed just to fantasize about making love to beautiful women. My fondest memory was thinking I was a trout, having sex with this waitress who was another trout. I picked up a lot of subtle things the ordinary person might never stop to dwell on.

I take two pills a day and the rest of the day I feel pretty normal. If I didn't take the pills, the fantasies and grandiose ideas would come rushing back and convince me that is the way things really are.

The fantasies were enjoyable, but there were a lot of letdowns too. I would never have real things happen to me. Now more tangible things can happen, like sitting here talking to you. I think it's a good trade-off.

Poverty is the most painful symptom of mental illness. A person has to eat and have clothes and keep clean. A lot of mentally ill people don't have those things. I do, because I played ball with the system. Even if I do have paranoid schizophrenia, I'm a success on certain terms. The system does have some winners.

1984
world champions
I'M
A
SURVIVOR

Joyce Kasinsky

My parents were commies, and when I was a child the FBI would come to the door. I think that was where my paranoias originated.

My dad died in 1966 and we moved. I spent a lot of time packing stuff, and I guess people were talking about me. I thought there were people who would shoot me from the rooftops.

I was visiting a psychiatrist. She said, "Why don't you go and check out this hospital." I said, "Jesus, at least while I'm in there they won't be able to shoot me."

They had me on Thorazine and I developed migraine headaches that would last all day. I left the hospital with the intention of killing myself, but then I got outside and I felt no migraines.

My apartment is in a very small building and the landlord and manager sort of know that I'm sort of crazy. They treat me as though I'm unaware of things and generally dumb. It bothers me immensely. My income is from social security disability and it's not much. It's just depressing that I will have to spend forever in this place.

The nitty gritty stuff that goes on in your life day-to-day—how difficult that can be for somebody who's out, even for somebody who's been out for some time. One time I had this enormous temptation to present myself in the emergency room and say, "Take care of me." I didn't do that, and I'm very proud of myself.

My biggest fear is that they'll call the cops and cart me away. One morning I couldn't find my glasses, and I was running around the apartment screaming. So the cops were at my door, and I thought, "Oh my God, this is it." They told me they thought someone was hurting me. "I'm not crazy, I just lost my glasses." I said it about seventeen thousand times. It's just that hideous fear because you've been there.

Jim Crotty weighed 145 pounds when I first photographed him, a few months after he left the hospital. He had entered the hospital at 112 pounds. He is over 6 feet tall.

Jim Crotty

The thing with food is that I was looking for a great explanation. When I was down it was, "Oh, too much sugar, that's the problem."

When I first went to the hospital I was so thin, so weak. They said I've got an eating disorder. Wow, now I know what I've got. Eat the right food and that takes care of everything.

In the hospital—"Rah, rah, Jim, you ate all the food on your tray." I felt great! I got to the point where I was gaining weight, but I was still sad. I discovered that I'm angry, extremely angry. And then I was bawling my head off. I get angry when I want to cry, and I cry when I want to be angry.

I think I'm the type who does look for the great overall explanation. I had all these ideas about proper diet, but I became nuts. It was crazy to want to starve myself.

The eating disorder is a mask for other sadness. I didn't want to acknowledge the real changes that would have to go on. I always wanted to be different and special—I eat this way so I'm different than you. Letting go of that— it's hard. Right now it's tough because I'm still feeling lonely.

There's kind of a perverse pride in being able to get so thin. I was a freak. I'm not going to lose weight again. I've set a weight goal of 145, and even that's too low. I want to be much more than that.

Jim Crotty and *Michael Lane*

I met Jim Crotty again two years after our first interview. He was living with Michael Lane. Jim was present during the interview with Michael.

Michael

At the dance, I noticed when you walked into the room. You were incredibly beautiful—angular, sharp, yet a softness about your face and voice that was very inviting.

Within the first month two issues came up—sex and food. On the first evening that you opened up sexually with me, suddenly you went to the kitchen to eat and left me in your bedroom.

I was afraid. In fact, I was terrified to acknowledge this was real. I had thought, O.K., you had gotten thin, you went to the hospital, and now you're out. But that evening was a jolt. You were confused about where things came from—affection, food.

You'd serve dinner and the portions were so tiny, and you would say, "If you really chew each bite you don't need to eat that much." I said, "We're two 6 foot guys. We can't live on these portions no matter how much we chew." Then suddenly you'd announce you had overeaten. I would look at you and laugh. I just couldn't get it.

In the beginning I would touch you and hug you, because of the confusion about food and love. But then I lost patience. I felt that you could just stop it, halt the craziness. Finally, I'd say, "Get off it, get out of the kitchen."

I started seeing you improve within the first months we were together. I was understanding it more, believing it is very real for you. When we met you were weak and depleted, and today you're feeling healthy and have energy. A lot has changed.

Food still holds a power over us. There's still pain around it, but it's fading away. Food can feed our love, so we can be together.

Wade Fisher

In my family I'm seen as the mainstay, the main mast, the masthead. It was overwhelming so I went to the hospital.

They sent me to a halfway house. I was encouraged to continue with my teaching—substituting high-school English, history, and science. And, I don't know if I should say this, I was having hallucinations, exuding evidence of self-persecution.

If there's a lot of people in a close environment, I have to bolt, I have to exit, I have to go. Also, oh God, people can read my thoughts. I have to control my thoughts to pleasant thoughts. You don't want other people to hear your bad thoughts, think you're such a reprobate, such a lout.

Sometimes I project as being kind of weird, like I'm standing on one foot. Today I was called in to teach, and I travel on the train, and people can hear my thoughts. Here I am dressed in business attire, and I feel like—an idiot. But I just think back on how difficult it was to get my degree, and I look the devil into the eye and charge right ahead.

A lot of people think I'm well and sometimes I see the problem going away. But sometimes it comes back, like a roaring from the dark lagoon. They say if you receive therapy on a five year continuum, whatever the problem was, it will go away. I've been in therapy four years.

Darryl Del Monte

My first marriage—one day it was over. I just fractured. Anxieties were all jumping around my head. I signed myself in.

After about a year, things started going good. I met this gal, and we were going to be married. I got a job working with attack dogs. It was becoming primeval, as if I was canine in my own way. I started plotting to let the dogs loose. That's when I caught myself. I thought, my God, I got to get some help. And I went apart again.

I'm on lithium now. That's the whole crazy thing. I should have been on lithium a long time ago. All of these years I've just had my mind shattered by these highs and lows. This is the first time I have direction.

I've had a hell of a time trying to find work. I went in and said, "Look, I'm a hard worker, and I'm a manic depressive." They said, "If you've got something like that, you're at the bottom of the list, man." Like what am I, some kind of freak? People are going to run away, shouting, "Manic depressive, manic depressive, get out of here, quick!"

The medication only holds back so much. Recently we were living on welfare, and it wasn't enough. There were fights. I would keep after her, slamming away, and she'd slam back. Having no job, and the financial pressure, it was overriding the medication.

I'm seeing a psychiatrist now who's tremendous. I feel like I'm speaking to somebody with an intellect who's recognizing that I have the same.

David Corson

Dad was an Air Force pilot. When he wasn't sleeping he was flying, so that we could keep alive. I had to find the nearest available father figure and it was Captain Kirk. Kirk's always in command. I try to emulate how he remains in control. That's how things should go with my life.

I'm 27. Have you ever wondered why I'm not married? I know why. I've got my father's anger still inside me. I respect women too much to be able to risk that anger will come flying out, just as it did with Dad.

I remember a terrible fight—my mother's voice calling for help. Can you imagine what it's like? I was the only one I could think of who was doing that to my father. The thing to do was ask to be put in one more hospital. Hell, any old port in a storm.

I realized I had that same potential in me to be violent. I promised nobody would ever get hurt out of my anger. And nobody's been hurt. I can get pretty dirty sometimes, but I would never use fists.

I rarely let go of my emotions until I'm sure somebody can take my anger without falling apart. If I lose control of my Command I'm lost. I have to remind myself of that incident between Dad and Mom.

Let me tell you one thing—I'm loyal. Anybody that takes a potshot, fist-wise, at any of the staff here—they've got to go through The Captain first. The need, thank God, has never arisen.

This area's going to be the first place hit in a nuclear war. I'm going to move to a small town, to where my parents live. That way I'll be out of the blast zone.

SANYO
STEREO CASSETTE

Laurie Roseman

I consider myself recovered. I take my lithium and I don't screw around. I abused amphetamines and activated something in my brain that made it malfunction. The lithium has put it back in order. Hey, I'm a young woman. I'm 26 and I'm O.K. But I did lose five years.

My first experience was when I was 19. All I know is that I was getting on highs where I was going psychotic and the police would come. I assumed I was just imagining things and it would never happen again. But I kept getting nervous breakdowns—six hospitalizations. My last one was over a year ago and the doctor put me on lithium. I'm convinced. I swear by lithium.

I moved to a halfway house. When you live in a halfway house you're not really a full functioning adult. I stayed seven months.

I don't think I've healed all the way yet. But a lot of the problems—I'd probably have them anyway. I go to a psychiatrist, but so do lots of people. I have trouble with men, but not marked up to mental illness. I get depressed over money, but how could I say I'm mentally ill because I'm upset about money?

I really sat in a room for two years—just barely went out to get food. Coming from that to where I am now I've become a very strong person. The love and confidence from my family made a tremendous difference. My goal is to completely remove myself from the mental health system. I can make it.

I'd be scared to death not to take my lithium. The problems of going into the hospital are behind me.

Donald Gordon

I've not been in a mental hospital since Yale in 1947. I got to reading Nietzsche, and I had this deep religious and emotional conflict. One night I thought, I'm tired, I'm going to sleep. That was March, and I didn't come back to consciousness until November. They say I'd gone without clothes to the chapel and was screaming at the icons. They gave me electroshock—the total number was 37. It certainly helped erase my memory.

My first conscious recall was seeing a woman, down the hallway, screaming and waving her arms. But this electroshock creates passivity. What could I do? I had a bed and went to community meals and sat around, like a thing pushed along by the stream of events. Then suddenly a switch was clicked and my memory came back. What is this? Why am I in this hospital?

I went to college and graduated and went looking for a job. They said, "Oh yes, we'll employ you. But you skipped this thing on the form about previous mental illness." So I filled it in— treatment for schizophrenia, electroshock. And they said, "The door's over there." I kept getting beat, and beat, and beat.

Right now they say I'm crazy enough to get money for my craziness. I go to therapy groups to keep the government $185 coming in. I'll say this—if this president of the United States is sane, in contact with the reality of this world, then I'm happy to be insane. He has his phony Christianity, but he hurts people, cutting disability funds. Most of us don't see the people he's actually killing—grinding them up.

12/87

Mario Landa

In 1968 I was quite hyper. Alcohol eased that so I drank a lot. Six months later, the lows started coming in.

I had depression days where I couldn't make it to work. I didn't shave, I didn't bathe, I didn't eat very much. I stayed in bed for days.

I was sent to the hospital and they gave me 14 shock treatments. They wheeled me to a place like an operating room and put a mask on my face, and I went off. I woke up in a room with an attendant, and I was all tied up. After the shocks, I forgot a lot of things about my childhood which I treasured. It has never come back. The depression and anxiety went, and I came out O.K.

Several months after the shock treatments I came back to my depressions. Back to the hospital. Another 14 shock treatments. I got very discouraged. I asked God to help me with my depressions, but nothing came through. I just wanted to die. I went back to the hospital because I had taken an overdose.

The doctor gives me prescriptions to keep me going. We have classes to know about our drugs and their side effects. This one is good for anxiety and for mental fuckups. The side effects have to do with sex. You have a tremendous urge to come, but nothing comes out. This is not a problem for me because I have a side effect pill. The only side effect I have is saliva coming from both sides of my mouth.

I feel that the illness has increased. It makes me feel real bad. I'm a clean person, and I don't shave for over two weeks, and I'm in bed, and the room stinks. I don't know why this thing came to me.

Robert Fennell

To the Editor: June 5, 1983

As you can see from my enclosed FBI records, I was arrested for vagrancy in Berkeley in 1963, falsely charged with threatening President Johnson; i received international headlines and was imprisoned.

In Feb. 1964 i received a trial which determined that i was in fact mentally ill. I escaped and the Secret Service found me and placed me in the state hospital. In 1968 i escaped and went into hiding.

After several years of radical theorizing, i was able to intertwine communist theory with feminist theory, marxism with solanisism, in a very unique and radical fashion. However, after 13 years now, i've never been able to get anybody to join up with me. Still trying and, in my frustration, still turning to thoughts of assassination and revolutionary suicide.

Best wishes from the Feminist Church of Dialectical Sexism

Robert Fennell

April 3, 1986

Dear Lonny,

The cancer isn't causing me much pain, but the prognosis is still about a year to live.

Perhaps I can get my stuff together and fly out to S.F. for the opening of your exhibit from this book. Do you catch a lot of flak for including me?

Perhaps I can help promote your exhibit by jumping off the Golden Gate Bridge with only our correspondence in my pocket. But, if nothing else works, I can pick up the phone, call the Secret Service, and threaten the President. At any rate, I wish you all the best of luck.

Bob Fennell—schizo scholar in residence.

April 23, 1986

Dear Lonny,

Thanks for the phone call. I didn't mean to worry you.

HINCKLEY
FOR
PRESIDENT
He's had a shot
at the man. . .
Let's give him a
shot at the job.
And Jodie for Vice.
Hinckley for President Campaign c/o 1338 Haight St., SF, CA 94117
Born Again Lesbian

Sam Watts

They say I ended up pushing a boy down a flight of stairs and killing him. They locked me up, for manslaughter. I was seven years old, and I didn't get out until I was eleven.

A year later my father was giving me a whuppin' for something, and I tried to burn down the house. I was thirteen and I was going through so many extremes that I committed myself.

When I get too much pressure I get a pain that goes shooting up the back of my neck. When that happens I black out. I don't remember what I did, where I was, or anything. People say I just go plain nuts. I get this extraordinary pain and I just go crazy.

I lived on the streets for two years and I couldn't handle it. I could eat every night at the Food Project, but to find a place to sleep was the hardest thing in the world. The cops find you at three in the morning and they say, "Go somewhere we can't find you." I said, "Yeah, that'll be fine," and I went back to the state hospital.

I'm just losing it. My friends are actually holding me more together than myself. I'm too rambunctious and it's caused me a lot of pain. I think I'm nuts, man. I don't have a cold heart, it's just some mornings I wake up on the wrong side of the bed. If I let it go .... I don't feel like talking about it.

There's going to be over a hundred thousand crazy people on the streets because of Reagan's cuts. It's going to get harder for people to survive and it's going to drive everybody nuts.

Jan Hamerquist

Paranoia is off and on, you know. Sometimes if I don't get enough sleep, or if I use drugs, it can initiate it.

Paranoia is the most difficult thing. Like if a person sounds depressed on the radio—it's my fault. But I'm fortunate, I'm able to pass out of it.

In the hospital I take the medication, I get some sleep, and I get some food in my body. I'd rather not be using medication, but I don't like being crazy.

This July I was living with my mate and child. When I got a blowout it was really a strain on her. While I was in the hospital she hooked up with some other guy, so that was very horrible. Right now I don't feel exactly at my best. I feel at my best when I'm playing with my daughter, feeding her, changing her diapers. Me and her were pretty tight.

Mostly I've been sleeping on the streets. It's an economic thing. I've been sending money for the child's care.

I've been on government disability since '76, and sometimes I dream of paying them back. I'd like to say I have control over my life, but I don't seem to understand exactly how to change.

I need to feel like I'm doing something worthwhile. If I start to live in a place I feel good about, get involved in some work activities, I'd feel comfortable then. Feeling better about myself would make it easier for someone else to care about me. I'm sure some of the craziness would go away.

Karen Moore

When you're psychotic it's a world of me, me, me. My last breakdown was fun. I was convinced this attractive person had hidden cameras and he was putting me on T.V. When they took me to the hospital I felt terribly deprived of a private moment.

I was so overcharged I thought I was a walking atom bomb. I remember screaming and thinking, my God, is that my voice? Where is this coming from? I thought I had lost my soul.

Outside the hospital, you're checking yourself a lot to see — is that a normal reaction or is that a little off? Last week there were three people at work and all at once they went to the supervisor's room. I was alone, thinking, well, should I be paranoid or not?

I enjoy my psychotic states. It's a total freedom. All of your fantasies come true. Barry Manilow was on T.V. and I was sure he was looking at me. I want more experiences like that. If I didn't have to support myself, I'd stop my medications and just experience it.

I want to be psychotic again sometime. You strip bare this rotten personality and rebuild a new one. When I'm psychotic I get total emotional release. I'm expressive, but it's to this imaginary audience. That's the sad thing.

Brandie Johnson

I had broken into people's houses and was dressing up in women's clothes. My mother was convinced I was crazy and should be locked up, so I was in the hospital from age 16 to 23. There's a lot of blank spaces because the shock treatments affected my memory.

I had some homosexual relationships with older men. I was a kid and didn't know much, so I dealt with it by saying it never did occur. Only it did. And it's left scars. I'm afraid of sex, and I don't relate to men too well. I'm a lesbian.

I've never felt male even though I was, physically. But I had trouble making up my mind. I'd throw away all my clothes and start dressing male again. Next thing I know I'm starting to sneak women's clothes and buy makeup. I went through it 10 or 15 times before I finally said, "The hell with this. I'm a woman."

I was very unsure of myself sexually so I had no lovers. I was afraid I wouldn't be doing it right, or I'd be laughed at, so I didn't try. It was very frustrating.

I don't use labels any more. Whether I'm top or bottom or switch, I'm a person first. Anything else is secondary. I predict myself as a live-in French maid to a mistress. I want adventure. I won't be stuck doing the housewife bit.

Leonard Bradley

When I was eight years old they said I had a thing—what do you call it, when you light fires and stuff? They kept me in the hospital for two years. I got out when I was ten and my stepfather beat me up real bad. The neighbors heard it, and the next day the sheriff came by and asked me if I wanted to go into the Youth Home. I said, "Yeah, sure I'll go. I'm scared to shit of my stepfather."

I had homosexual tendencies and I started playing around with my brother. They had me put in the state hospital and it was really neat. I learned how to square dance, and I was in a little play at Christmas. They had these rich society ladies come on your birthday and this real nice lady would give you this box of chocolates. My stepfather came to visit me, and he was in tears. He says, "What I done is really evil," and he brought me some shoes.

I ran away and took a bus to Miami. I was going to be a hustler on the beach. I met this young man that was going to Yale and he liked me and he took me to dinner and I had veal scallopini. We lived together for a week or so, but we weren't compatible.

The last time I was hospitalized was three years ago. I was using drugs a lot, injecting methedrine, and I just got burned out and went to the hospital. I was still having problems then. Drugs were maybe part of them. I've been off the street these three years, but I still have a drug problem. When I was eight years old they were popping pills in my mouth. I like doing drugs.

I've been seeing the same psychiatrist for eight or nine years. He's really a nice doctor. We have group therapy every Monday. Today we're supposed to have a picnic.

Brad Lichtenstein

I was going to be a rabbi and I began to look at my spiritual self. In a magical moment I stepped out of reality and felt myself above my body. It was the beginning of all things—the essence of all things.

The spirituality grew stronger. One evening I had a spontaneous writing from God. Every 2100 years there is a being who occupies the earth and brings enlightenment. The writing said I was that being.

Finally, I just let it all out. I said, "I am the Messiah. I need to deal with why people are starving." I began speaking of the second coming of Christ, and I was in the hospital that afternoon. The diagnosis was schizophrenia, thought-voices.

They began to talk to me as if I were a child. They took my clothes and I had to put everything into a locked box. From my huge position of the Messiah, I was degraded to being less than a person.

The medicine cut off the voices immediately. I was impressed. But I was still the Messiah. I've had too many profound experiences to not believe I am the Messiah.

Our socialization says that you don't talk on buses and you don't say you're the Messiah. The last time I told my doctor I still thought I was the Messiah, he said, "Take some more tranquilizers."

The voices are gone. I have a good job now. But if they say it is bad to think you are the Messiah then they haven't cured me. I can't lose God's message that I am on the right path.

Diane

I was so depressed it was hard to even function. I thought I would either hitchhike across the country or go into the hospital. My therapist suggested that I go into the hospital.

The doctor talked more with my therapist than to me. They decided I should be there for six weeks. I didn't want to stay that long, but he said if I didn't he would have me committed.

The doctor used me for a case presentation. They all gathered to make decisions about my future. I didn't want to be there and was standing there thinking, so the doctor turned to the audience and said, "She's trying to control us with her silence." I thought it was pretty ironic that he accused me of trying to control them. So I walked out.

I went back to the ward and I broke some windows. I had never done anything like break a window before I came to the hospital.

When I got out, my doctor put me on Stelazine. I could hardly walk from the drugs—my eyes wouldn't focus, and I couldn't do any work. I became desperate. I wanted to start megavitamin therapy, but my doctor told me it was poppycock. I found a megavitamin doctor and it took three months, but it worked! Things weren't so cloudy any more. I started getting more energy.

Recently, I've had various volunteer jobs, but they never last long. I volunteered to take care of dogs at the SPCA. One dog had been abused. He would just stare and not respond at all. I spent a lot of time with him and he started to respond.

Now I do things in between the depressions so that when they come on I already have my basic things together. Things come in cycles. It's hard to tell at this time what part of the cycle I'm in.

Dossie Easton

I was 20 and sexually active and I was not having orgasms. I kept trying—men, women, groups. I read the Freudian literature, that frigidity was a mental illness, a neurosis. Frigid women are hysterical. And I would occasionally get really upset and sit and cry. So the inorgasmia and hysterical attacks led me to seek help.

My therapist told me I didn't want to be a woman. Until I was ready to submerge my identity in a relationship I would not have orgasms and I would be mentally ill.

They wanted me to be in this prep school funny farm, so for three months I stagnated in the hospital. Then I started masturbating and having orgasms. I became more self-confident, and I've never had a hysterical attack again.

I found out my diagnosis was schizophrenia. You've got fantasies, day-dreams, wet dreams? You must be psychotic. So they fed me Thorazine and I realized these people could actually hurt me. So I left.

A friend opened the San Francisco Sex Information Switchboard, and I worked doing feminist sex counseling. I finished my degree in human behavior, and now, 20 years down the line, I'm working with people who went to the hospital just like me.

I remember people used to say, "Dossie, you need to love yourself more." Masturbation is how I learned to have orgasms, and that gave me the self confidence I needed to take control of my life. If anything made a difference it was the discovery of feminism, and the validation of my sexuality.

Joan Scroggs

I was 2 years old and remember saying, "Am I a boy or a girl?" My mother said, "Well, you're a boy of course." And this immense feeling came over me—something is terribly wrong. I prayed I would wake up some morning and be a girl.

I started going steady in high-school and, in a very innocent childhood exploration, she got pregnant. I was 17 and we got married. We were married for 27 years.

I told her I had this fascination to wear girl's clothes. She didn't want to talk about it, even got violent. So it was held for 27 years in utmost secrecy within my heart.

Six years ago my wife left. My children were grown, my wife gone—I had a right to live *my* life.

I've worked in broadcast engineering for 30 years. I was on vacation and had it announced that I'd be returning to work as a woman. It's been a tremendous stress on me—to walk down the halls and be Joan, when they've known John for 30 years.

Do you understand the futility of where I am? I want to have been a little girl. The best I can ever hope to be is a very good imitation.

There comes a point, unconsciously, when you give up. Ten weeks ago I had this terrible feeling of despair and took a bottle of sleeping pills. In the hospital I suddenly realized I had been admitted as a female—and it was the most beautiful thing that ever happened to me. I got up in the morning as a woman, went to breakfast as a woman. I was there for two weeks and I didn't want to leave.

I make $40,000 a year and I'm in good health. Most people would say, "My God, you've got everything." I don't have a damned thing. The number one thing in our lives is sexual identity, and if nature tampers with that it can lead to despair.

The operation is only a tiny piece of the whole program. Things will be rearranged, reshaped, and put back the way they should have been. Once I have my operation I am no longer a transsexual. When you leave that hospital you are a woman.

Vernon Parker

I was doing good. I can't remember how long. You want me to talk like that, right? I lost my job because I was nervous. It was like I was in a fantasy world. Like maybe if I had a wife, maybe I'd feel better. My mother took me to a doctor and that was my first hospitalization.

It was kind of depressing to be in there 'cause all the women were crying. Maybe that's what it was. I'm trying to think. It's a feeling of losing rights—not rights, losing manhood—not manhood. I get a lot of opinions. Like,—paranoid. No, that's not a good one. It's hard to remember.

I think it's a feeling of helplessness. Is that a good answer? Yeah, helplessness. Well—can I change the answer? It's almost— almost as if I get withdrawn.

I'm on Haldol. It works for me. I was off it once and I got real antsy. It makes me think slower. I'm trying to think—I know what you're asking. People are too logical, not feeling enough.

Sometimes I feel like somebody's watching me. I mean like in government, spy things. Like I'm important for some reason to somebody.

Margaret House

Being crazy and being labelled crazy are two different things. The label is more of a problem. In grade school, kids called me a mental case.

When I was 22 my mind really did break. After a fight with my lover I thought he might be sending his friends to harass me. Things were rearranged in my apartment. Pages were missing from my journal. I got very frightened and moved out. I believed some people around me were warlocks. I stayed in this belief system for a whole year, and then I stopped believing it. I was 23 years old and I came out of it.

But I had some more actual violations and went back into the belief system. My parents committed me involuntarily and I spent seven weeks in the psychiatric ward. They had four staff grab me, throw me on a bed, pull my pants down, and give me a shot. I was pleading with them not to do it. I didn't fight like the stereotype of mental patients but went limp in the tradition of political activists.

During these active phases I'm somewhat more afraid than I have reason to be. On the other hand, I've had things happen that have shown me there are no limits to the violations this society will do to me.

Last summer I was running in the street and the police handcuffed me and took me to the hospital. I would lose my job and my apartment if they forced me to stay, so I convinced them I was rational enough to go home. They sent me home on the buses. I was afraid of everyone. The next day I met with a friend and realized she wasn't plotting against me. That brought things back to normal.

In the past, these active phases have led to my being committed. Now I'm used to them. I know better than to talk about what I'm thinking with people who might commit me. I prepare in advance in case something happens. I'm the lucky one-half of one percent as far as being this crazy and having this much control over my life.

TO HELL WITH THEIR PROFITS
STOP FORCED DRUGGING
DRUGGING
Save Energy...

Bob Weikert

If you know where you're coming from and you're not bothering anybody or going against the law, you can have a lot of fun being crazy. But if it happens off the wall it can be pretty depressing.

I was in this hotel and I was totally frustrated and I wasn't taking my medication and I freaked out. So I started a fire. Doesn't sound very rational, but I wasn't feeling very rational.

I remember times I was in the hospital, they had dances and things. But a hospital is a hospital. It's behind closed doors. I don't see myself going back. I'm just too strong these days.

I was sent out under psychiatric care to this board and care house. I like it here. I have my own keys and I get my medicine. Mrs. W has a good heart—gave me six pairs of socks last Christmas. I've been here three years and I see my probation officer for the last time a week from today. In October the charges are dropped and I'm free to go.

I go to the Creative Living Center—for people with mental illness. I'm in the work program. You crack walnuts for a place that buys them. My psychiatrist told me to do more things, so I moved to "house and grounds," and I'm glad. They elected me supervisor, which means I make the coffee and tea. I'm handling more responsibility.

The medication stabilizes me. The other part is peace of mind, and a decent lady. I'm getting stronger every day, and I'm going to make the most of myself. Things are finally going my way.

I still hear voices sometimes. I haven't figured out where they're coming from. I don't want to discuss it.

I get along with the program, I take my medicine, I eat proper. There's not going to be no more relapses. I've suffered enough. That's about all I have to say for this interview.

Dennis Mason

Because I'm blind they think I'm more desperate. You know, that I need them. I don't.

I went to the state hospital for the drug program. I was shooting Nembutal, codeine, whatever I could get my hands on. I was taking pills like M&Ms.

You're willing to do anything to get more drugs. I've ripped off pills, money, people's old ladies. You go to bed with anyone, you're that strung out. There's this pimp down in Delano. Well, say a woman would come in and she'd want a guy? There were three of us, we used to wear jumpsuits, and she'd say which one she wanted.

I've gone to bed with the ugliest and the grossest women for money. They wanted sex, I wanted drugs. The dope I get now, well, usually it's given to me by broads because I've gone to bed with them.

These women turn my stomach. Any broad that has to give a guy drugs or money to go to bed with them, they're just not worth it.

Taking drugs makes me less nervous. I'm, let's say, more liberal. I'm more me. I'm planning to cut down on drugs, you know, not severely, but so much at a time. A lot of people, when they're taking drugs, do things and say things that are not necessarily so.

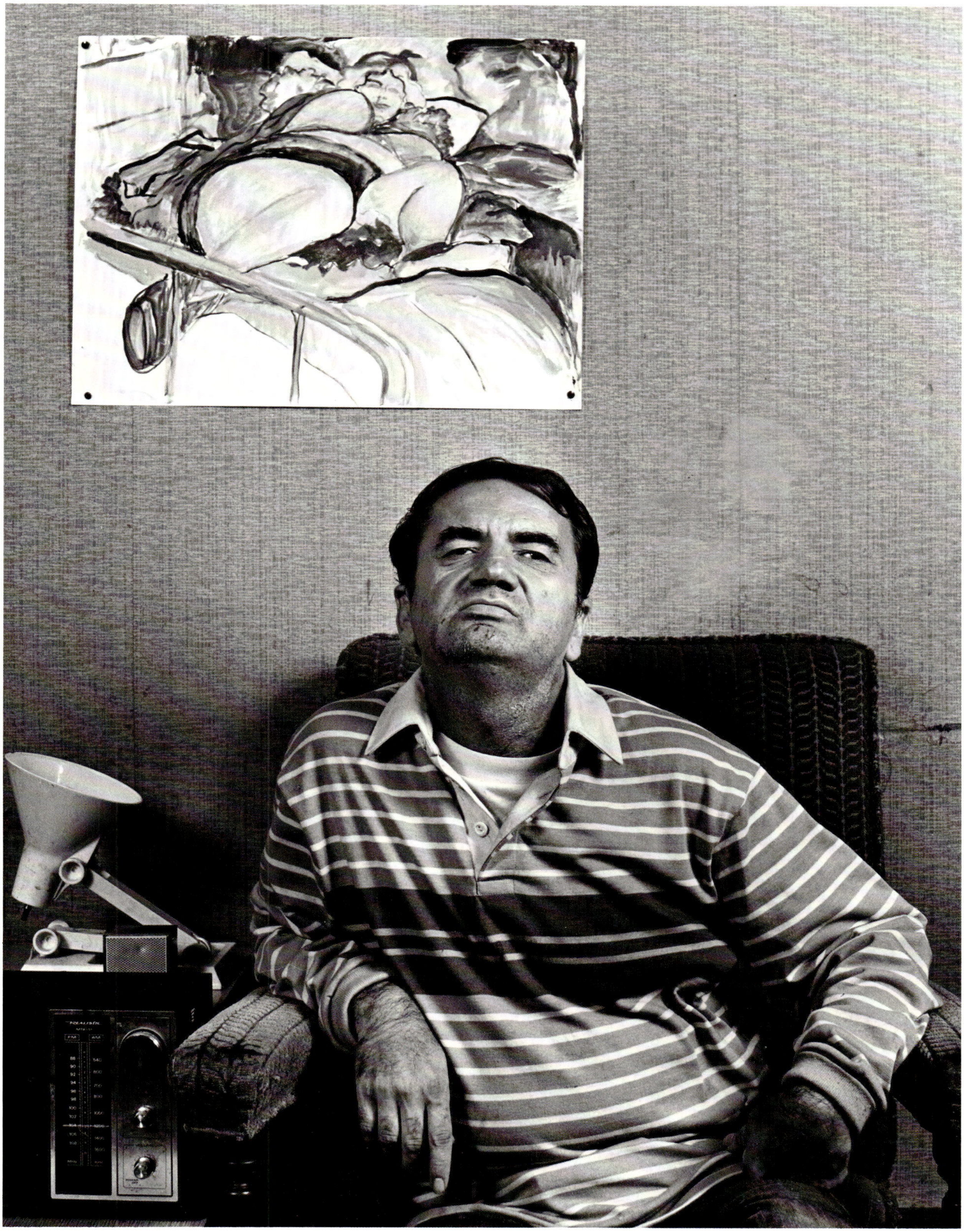

Barbara Bair-Nichols

I always knew that God loves me intensely, although I thought He was a little nutso for having my mom beat me. Chances are someday He's going to heal me.

From age five I can remember being severely beaten. I figured she was sick and couldn't help it, and I was no good. But I wasn't going to be mad at God because then He'd have her kill me.

The whole 15 years I did 30 or 40 suicides. I was using combs to do my wrists, anything. I'd make suicide attempts even while I was in the institutions. If I died, they'd know that I meant it, and they didn't love me good enough.

They diagnosed me as schizophrenic. I knew schizo meant seriously long-term sick and I was terrified. If you go to a state hospital, that's it. You're there forever. What I did was become quiet and passive. I did whatever they said, so I was only there for two weeks.

After my last severe attempt to kill myself,in 1980, I woke up from a coma and knew that God had saved my life. I made a commitment that I would never overdose again. And it's not that I kept that commitment so extraordinarily beautiful, but they were minor—like 12 non-prescription tablets.

I was in psych emergency service in 1983 for a minor suicide attempt. I brought my teddy bear with me because I feel so at their mercy. They said they want my bear, but I was scared and wouldn't give it to them. If they'd explained they sometimes get stuffed animals with guns in them and they had to search the bear for weapons I would have let them. But five people attacked me and dug their nails in and I was bleeding. I got my bear back, but I was so terrified by their reaction that it was a real turning point for me.

I never ever want to be so vulnerable that I have to be physically restrained again. That is the basis of my recovery. It's just a miracle. The Lord and I worked so hard at eliminating the daily depressions that I cannot remember the emotional pain and self-hate of wanting to kill myself. I'm happy to be alive. And it's not like it's easy to be happy. I just can't believe He would permit me to die before age 99.

Clementina Thirty-Seven

My diagnosis is adjustment disorder, which means I don't fit in. For any intelligent human being that's a sign of a healthy spirit. I resist the insanity we live in.

I was a successful young artist, published in *Saturday Evening Post,* and my posters were sold internationally. But I got ripped off for $10,000 and I fell in love and moved deep into the woods. I became so isolated and reclusive I lost touch with reality.

I got on government disability for a mental disorder. I went to the court hearing dressed as a bag lady. I brought chocolate bunnies to smear across my face—I knew they wanted to see me drooling. In some countries the government supports artists, so I can respectfully say I'm being funded to do my work. I have a vision, and I don't call that a mental disorder.

I have uncommon knowledge that needs to be shared. Here's an article about my last major show, "Memoirs of a Primitive Woman in Exile." I am responsible to educate people and share my experiences.

Two years ago I spent three solid months packing all the things I make. I put my life into storage. I couldn't see anything but darkness. I was put on medication to see me through. And I pulled through.

There are those that are labelled crazy that in fact are teachers. We all know that crazy artists die and then become famous. I will reach people before I die, in my time. If in 20 years my name is out there, remember I told you this was to be.

Judi Chamberlin

Vivian Bard

Even my mother's called the police on me. That hurts. You have a problem, they lock you up—give you pills when you need food and a place to stay.

I was 23, a mother, a father, and a full-time employee. I was tired, kind of having hallucinations, quoting the Bible. It led to the psychiatric ward.

At medication time they rang a little bell, "Medication, take your medication." You had the medication and you made your bed, and the rest of the day you're just watching T.V. and walking up and down the halls.

One thing I found very difficult to take was the restraints. It was a very horrible experience to be in restraints, tied down, no bedpan, nothing. It haunts me.

I thought I would never go back. I tried working part-time but had hallucinations, voices. They shipped me to the state hospital. They had dances on Saturdays. But you can't be very close to the males, even though you're grown. I was there for nine months.

I'm always going to have to take medication. Always going to face the possibility of being locked up, in restraints, hospitalized, low self-esteem, thinking of suicide, insomnia, heavy smoker, drinking coffee by the pot.

This year I was hospitalized again. I was pregnant with my second son and I was by myself. I ended up on the streets and the police found me at two in the morning. Back to the hospital. Take your medicine and watch T.V.

It was really difficult because I wanted the baby to make it. My man had nothing to give the baby. Not one diaper.

I thought the baby should be in a foster home. It took a lot out of me. My man was very angry with me for doing it. He felt so hurt. I tried to explain to him that it's a temporary thing.

Kayo Harris

I'm a manic depressive. I'm 70 years old and I'm like a time bomb.

I was a very active photographer, but I started doing crazy things. Telling you this is just stirring me up.

In '65 I took a little Lysol. Screwed up my throat. Let's take a break here. I was hyped before you came. Now I'm twice as hyped. I have to keep moving.

I'm going high and I'm going low, like a monkey on a stick. When I'm hyper I run from place to place. I'm awake at 3 in the morning and I sweat it, man.

They had me taking pills like candy. Listen, I think I'm beyond drugs. I go to a mental health clinic. The guy there says to me, "Today is the first day of the rest of your life." I need a neurosurgeon and I get a philosopher.

How long can I go on like this? How long before I really flip? There are no miracle pills and there are no miracle speeches. I'm exhausting myself. I'm an old man, you know.

What am I trying to go so fast for? You've got lots of tape. What am I going to do when you leave, take up needlepoint?

Jo Ann Dailey

I owned a massage parlor, and the police lieutenant had warned me. He said, "Jo Ann, if I see another man come out of that place smiling, I'm going to get you." I believe it was the police that burned it down.

I had no income and no place to live. So I went for a walk, a three month walk. I had voices in my ears and it was coming out of my teeth. "Don't worry about it, don't worry about it," over and over again. I ate fruit off the trees and out of the garbage pail at McDonald's. My children put out a missing persons thing on me and they put me in the hospital.

I didn't mind the hospital and I didn't mind the food. I don't have the voices since I take my pills. I like it better this way.

I applied for government disability—SSI. I went to rent an apartment eight times, telling them I was on SSI, and they turned me down eight times. I finally lied and told them I had a job and I got this place. I worked at the school at yard duty, but SSI said that if you work steadily, regular, you will be cut off from your SSI. And you are not well, we can tell.

Once, I stopped taking my pills because it hurt my body too bad. I went for a long walk again. When you hear voices you listen to them tell you what you should do. I went back into the hospital again and they found a pill I could take.

Both of my girl friends wound up back in the hospital. Susie didn't take her pills for four or five months—and away she went.

David Charter

The violence started when I was 14. I was drunk and I was breaking all the windows. Anger—fuck you, go to hell. I was institutionalized for uncontrollable behavior. Something about paranoid schizophrenic. I don't know.

When I was 21 my wife wanted to divorce me and I just snapped. I had one of these big bear knives and I tried to kill her.

In jail they found I had a mental history. So my public defender said, "Plead guilty, go to the state hospital, and try to get your ass some help—or you go to San Quentin."

The hospital was a fear world. I've always needed to be in control. I woke up one night and the bed next to me was on fire and the guy was jumping around and screaming. I saw that I wasn't in control.

I had never been that low before. And this patient said, "Lookit, man, I can see right through you. You're not going to get anything out of life." He started me saying, "I need help."

There were people that could not care for themselves. I helped them cut their meats up, protected them, became a part of their lives. And that was the start of helping myself. I could keep what I'd learned about being a tough person away from me.

And there was Julia, one of the psych nurses. I had just come through this disastrous divorce and Julia was just starting her divorce. I was able to hear the woman's side of it, of two people bonded. We had a lot in common.

My social worker and doctor said, "Hey, we see you wanting to help yourself." And I saw myself caring. "O.K., let me go. I'm going to finally live." I was 25 and I had grown up.

I've been out two years but it's still a transition period. I mean, it's not just the 8 months in the state hospital, it's the 27 years of my life. I feel like, "Hey, I can change the damn world." I'm considering becoming a psych nurse. Sometimes I don't even believe myself, saying that. The physical and emotional violence is gone, and caring will keep it away.

Julia Detwiler *and* ***David Charter***

Julia works as a psychiatric nurse at the hospital where David Charter was a patient. *(See previous page.)*

Julia

We were always short-staffed and David helped the ones that weren't getting enough attention. Then, all of a sudden, he was quiet again. So I just started talking to him, and he got into the whole thing about why he was there. He was just an easy person to talk to.

I was going through a difficult time in my own life—ending a marriage of ten years. I have two children, and I didn't want to rip the family apart.

David was working so hard on getting his own life together. When you talk to someone who's hit rock bottom and is pulling himself up there's a lot of insight that can be shared. I recognized the pain David had gone through and became determined to straighten my own life out. We became close friends.

We talked every day. Then it was every minute we could snatch away. One day we handed notes to each other and both ran away. We had written love notes.

What precipitated it was David's getting ready to leave. I thought I'd never see him again. We were letting each other know there was life after the state hospital.

I was on vacation when he got out and we'd go for walks and sit for hours and talk. And by then we were kissing.

It was hell. It spread like wildfire through the hospital. Our relationship was growing stronger by the day, and the clinical director wanted my job. I began to believe, "Am I really doing something wrong here?" I would come home and cry and David would reassure me.

They said, "How can you be sure that David will be O.K.?" And I said,"There are no guarantees in anything, but I love him. He's been there just as much for me as I have for him."

People's attitudes do spill into our lives. We will always be open and honest about our situation and that opens us up for exploitation.

My life with David, a "psychotic mental patient," is ten times better than my marriage ever was. Dave's my best friend. If we get into conflict it's male and female stuff, not psych nurse and patient. We have no pretensions with each other.

People who are happy with themselves just see us and like us as people. Our life is probably better than most couples because we cherish what we have.

Theodore Paul Switzer

A real brother or sister will never lie, steal, cheat or deceive you, nor take unfair advantage of you. The church I run is a controversial church. I preach the laws.

I figured, I got spare time, I'll do some cancer research. I obtained a chemical analysis of tobacco smoke, and I said, "That's it." I went to Washington to get them to do something about it and I got nothing but the runaround. I got so pissed off I crashed my truck into the White House gate. Somehow, they sidestepped the issue of the tobacco and accused me of being mentally ill—paranoid personality, whatever that is.

Let's put it this way. Somebody is using the mental health system to get control over certain people. While I was locked up, the U.S. Forestry Service burned my house and church down. This is their method of silencing me. The tobacco companies might be behind it.

The court turned me loose just earlier this month. "No threat to society," they said. The Bible talks about freeing the prisoners, right? It's obvious I wasn't mentally ill.

Mark Greer

When you're young, like what do you call it, adolescent stage? I went through that and it took me the hard way. I blew my temper and I broke this guy's nose and that's how it all started.

I've got a temper problem. A temper problem is not a mental problem or a physical problem. It's a temper problem. I start yelling and cussing. I do O.K., except when I know I'm right and somebody says I'm wrong, it makes me upset.

My mother couldn't cope with my yelling and screaming. My father and I started punching each other out and my mother called the police and I was put in a home for broken-home people. It was unbelievable. There was a homosexual, gay, bisexual, heterosexual. I just got fed up with it so I moved, because I was supposed to get married with my fiancee. But she was telling a lot of lies, and her mother accused me of raping her, so I just let her go.

I moved here in 1981, and I've been here ever since. This is the best place you can stay in—Mrs. Wilson's family home, the best place. It's number one. I've been helping them, like brotherhood, you know, and fellowship, and stuff like that.

I go to Creative Living Center—a place for people that are mentally ill. Mrs. Wilson took me over there. I kept on trying, and kept on trying, and kept on trying. Finally, I got me a job. I'm an expert janitor now. I vacuum the rugs, the second floor, the stairs.

The thing is I'm going home in 1990, going back home. My mother's going to retire in 1990. I'm my mom's only son she's got. You ever heard of "your flesh and blood"? That's right. Between now and 1990 I'm just going to do the best I can. So that's about it right there.

Jesus
Never
Fails

Anne Boldt

My parents were very restrictive, so I never really learned how to take care of myself. I experimented with sex and drugs and got very unhappy. I made some suicide attempts.

I got to the point where I knew that cutting my wrists wouldn't kill me, but it was a release of energy to do it. The psychiatrist prescribed antidepressants, but they made me tired and I couldn't concentrate. I thought I was really going crazy.

I spent the next five years in and out of mental institutions. I went to the hospital so often because I was on welfare and lived in a place with rodents, and I couldn't afford to eat. So the institution was kind of pleasant.

I do have experiences where my being leaves my body and I float around the room. When I'm feeling frightened or angry I just leave my body. It gives me a break from feeling all the pain. My friends get real scared. My eyes are open, I don't blink, I don't respond. Once they actually picked me up to take me to a mental hospital, and I just started screaming, "No hospital!"

I'm really terrified of being in a mental hospital again. It took me years to get back my sense of self-worth and wanting to be alive. I don't trust myself to be strong enough to maintain my self-worth and dignity if I were locked up again. The last time I was in an institution was 12 years ago.

Everyone has the possibility to have out of body experiences. But people are so afraid that they block their ability. And when it does happen, they say it's a sickness. I wouldn't be at all concerned about it if I wasn't running the risk of being locked up.

Pat Moore

I'm a transsexual. I've been compensating all of my life through violence and hair-raising macho, but in socially acceptable ways, like Vietnam. After the war I went on to an illustrious career as a mercenary—Africa, Central America, Asia. I became a political assassin. It's a stable, sincere job for ex-military people.

One day, I allowed myself to relate to my needs as a transsexual. I leaned on the United States' social support bullshit, checked into a VA hospital and laid my story on the line. You can fake anything in the world and see what you get out of it, but there's a line where you lose control. People start putting labels on you. Last year I spent nine months in the hospital.

I never have been psychotic. The very longevity of my patient record gave them more latitude to label me with heavier and heavier diagnoses. The only solution was to conform a bit, go to work.

Now I'm in a rehabilitation program, studying computer science. I'm going to jump right into the mainstream of society, establish income, social and occupational credibility.

The system did nothing for my life except provide a free hotel. I'm going to live two distinct lives—the radical adversary of the mental health system, and this straight existence in the computer industry.

Sure I have chronic and intermittent depression. It comes from a lifetime of role suppression. I saturated my environment so heavily with macho shit to prove my masculinity. For a true transsexual, you cannot suppress it.

NEW TRAIL
7K9A32
GRAHAM & GRANOLA

Sally Zinman

What happened to me was a breakout, not a breakdown. I had reached my early thirties and had not been able to break from my parents. One day I woke up and I had no idea who I was. I told my father that he was a very nice man, but he wasn't my father. Two aides from the hospital showed up and said I had to go.

From 1970 to 1973 I was in a private hospital. The doctor, Rosen, did not use drugs and he did not use shock treatment. He beat his patients. He believed that psychosis could be scared out of a person.

They stripped my clothes off and tied my hands and beat me in the face and breasts. I escaped and called my parents. Rosen told them the beatings weren't real but were part of my paranoia. My father took me back. I was screaming, "Don't leave me here. You can't leave me here."

I escaped again. The first night was spent in a bathroom in a gas station. They found me and this time I was put in a cellar in my underwear and bra, with a bucket for a toilet, for two months. I could get out only if I told them who I was. But I didn't know. They conditioned me to say the name, but it wasn't me.

I didn't leave for two years. I couldn't go anywhere without them finding me. When Rosen finally allowed me to leave I decided I would find out who I really was. And I would do something about Rosen.

I hired a private investigator and we interviewed aides and past patients, tracing his pattern of beatings. In 1980, a patient had been beaten to death. The state came up with 101 charges, and the court took away his license.

Now I'm working for the Network Against Psychiatric Assault. We need a real alternative to the mental health system—one that is voluntary, run by peers, doesn't use drugs, and doesn't rely on intimidation.

The first day I was considered to be nuts was to me the first free day of my life. I created a person whose values and work I like.

I received this message on my answering machine one morning:

"This is Darwin. I understand you want to interview me. Be prepared to accept some anxiety, hostility, resistance. But I will respond to a knock on the door at 12:30."

The next message was also from Darwin:

"Oh, but I'm not dangerous. Good luck."

Darwin Dias

My name's Darwin, like the man who invented the monkey. I hit the planet in '34.

The last trip to the state hospital was in '66. I thought something was controlling me. I hadn't figured out it was in my own mind.

In the hospital the higher-ups with thick German accents pinned me down and questioned me. I told them they were full of shit. I was there for the treatment of my mental health, not to be harassed by the staff.

When I got out I looked into all kinds of esoteric philosophies and came upon the works of Sigmund Freud. I learned about the body of Freudian knowledge, and I psychoanalyzed myself. It opened my eyes to what this "mental illness" thing is.

Psychoanalytic thought is a compound complexification of knowing the dynamicism of how the unconscious mind works. I was able to find my own mind, which never happened in the state hospital with the behavioralist nerds.

My concern is for the people I see on the street. I know how they came down because I came down the same way. Mental health funding should be diverted from locked wards to community services, to help people get back to a lifestyle that's not such a nightmare. Being crazy is being the victim of mind-fuck situations all the time. If you beat a dog, you're going to turn it mean. The whole system is a madness machine.

THIS
PLACE
IS
BUGGED

Patty McFadden

I think it's the speech impediment that keeps me from being close to people. Plus my childlike simpleness.

I was four and I was tearing up things and biting other children, so I was sent to the state hospital. I had a super craving to be loved, but I was put away, like food storage. Later I went to the hospital again. It was depression and suicide.

I live in a boarding home now and I hope not to stay forever. They feed you mostly—I call it air—macaroni, and those instant potatoes. Anne's the best person to share a room with because she's so soft. She's really a fluffy person.

This other girl likes back rubs when she's sick, and I give them to her. But when I'm sick she's too busy. All of this anger built up and I threw a tennis racket through her window.

The church helps my heart to have more nourishment than I've gotten anywhere else. I like to go to church and things like that, but one on one, oh boy! I'm not able to put on that social mask that you see, where people look so perfect, and whole.

Dear Lonny,

I was not wholly honest in the interview. I can tell you that on paper now that I'm home.

My roommate is not fluffy. One day she likes me and another day she's disturbed because I stay home. The other girl I helped with back rubs, she returns it. She came and hugged me. She's hugged me a lot.

Boy you don't know how good I felt when you asked me for an interview. I was happy and awful terrified. I've been conditioned by so much criticisms from others. And always given advice, advice, and more advice. Then they get mad if I tell them, "There's a brain up here." I'm tired of all this unbearable loneliness.

Please can you forgive me? I am sorry.

Very Sincerely,

Patty McFadden

Marti Brokaw

It's only recently that I've actually made the statement, I am mentally disabled. I cannot have a job and make a living.

I lived with my family until I was 31. When they kicked me out I took some jobs—housekeeper, attendant. It was extremely painful. I was being exploited and degraded.

I have half a dozen misdemeanor convictions, for bashing windows, pouring paint on a police car. I was looking for a career place to live, but I couldn't get more than 60 days.

I've had fairly lightweight contact with the mental health system, on an open psych ward. I said, "Please, check me in, there's nowhere for me to go." And they did.

One year ago I walked out on the streets thinking I was going out there to die. But I got off the streets by walking into Support Services Shelter.

It's a refuge and a sanctuary in the women's dorm. Men confront me on the street all day and I have to defend myself. But they don't bother me at the shelter. These guys need that bunk.

I feel that my life is better being mentally disabled than if I was not. Everyone who's adjusted to manage in the world pays a price. Most people's jobs are really a matter of slavery. I will not permit myself to be degraded and abused.

I don't think I'm sick. It has to do with an integrity, and a self love.

41

AUTHOR'S AFTERWORD

"This is a memory book, rather than one of hard fact and precise statistics. It is an attempt to get the story. . . from an improvised battalion of survivors."
Studs Terkel
"The Good War"

"If I could tell the story in words, I wouldn't need to lug a camera."
Lewis Hine

I wanted to find a way around this insane public view of what crazy people are about—to slip by the media-propagated images of droolers, screamers, freaks, drugged-out zombies, psychotic killers and mind-scrambled lunatics. I needed to shed the protective armor of psychological jargon. Mostly, I wanted to overcome my own fear.

I looked for people who had been in mental institutions and, as word spread, they looked for me. I spent hour upon hour establishing trust (in both directions), talking, interviewing, photographing.

I've spent three years on this project, and I have no answers. But I am no longer afraid. And I have gained compassion for the large number of people who are different enough in this society to be called mentally ill.

I cannot, by skill, knowledge, or desire, enter the debate over the existence or non-existence of mental illness. I cannot change legislation or social policy, or even pretend to know what changes should be made. I leave to the patients, ex-patients, family members, mental health professionals, legislators and theoreticians the uncertainty and daily agony of these decisions.

The people who were willing to risk personal exposure in this book offer us the chance to hear the voices inside the experience of being "crazy." Their openness and desire to be heard allow us this glimpse of that vague and mysterious line of craziness that we have all approached, but only some have crossed.

Lonny Shavelson
Berkeley, California
August, 1986

A note about the interviews and portraits:

The interview with each person in this book lasted one to two hours. This interview was taped, and a transcription made from the tape. This was then edited to about two pages of what I felt was the crucial information that would be appropriate for the book.

In a second meeting, each subject and I reviewed the first editing and, together, wrote the final statement.

The portrait session followed immediately after this final editing. With the written statement still fresh in our minds, we discussed the message we wanted to convey in the visual image and made the photographs.